Lighting the Steps

T0098184

By Philip Holmes

Poetry

THREE SECTIONS OF POEMS
A PLACE TO STAND
THE GREEN ROAD

Applied Mathematics

NONLINEAR OSCILLATIONS, DYNAMICAL SYSTEMS
AND BIFURCATIONS OF VECTOR FIELDS
(with John Guckenheimer)

TURBULENCE, COHERENT STRUCTURES,
DYNAMICAL SYSTEMS AND SYMMETRY
(with John Lumley and Gal Berkooz)

CELESTIAL ENCOUNTERS: THE ORIGINS
OF CHAOS AND STABILITY
(with Florin Diacu)

KNOTS AND LINKS IN THREE-DIMENSIONAL FLOWS
(with Robert Ghrist and Michael Sullivan)

Philip Holmes

Lighting the Steps

Poems 1985–2001

ANVIL PRESS POETRY

Published in 2002
by Anvil Press Poetry Ltd
Neptune House 70 Royal Hill London SE10 8RF
www.anvilpresspoetry.com

Copyright © Philip Holmes 2002

ISBN 0 85646 339 6

This book is published
with financial assistance from
The Arts Council of England

A catalogue record for this book
is available from the British Library

The moral rights of the author have been asserted in
accordance with the Copyright, Designs and Patents Act 1988

Designed and set in Monotype Bell by Anvil
Printed and bound in England
by Cromwell Press, Trowbridge, Wiltshire

For Ruth, and for Maya, Avram, Ben and Ilana

Acknowledgements

I thank all those who offered advice, criticism and encouragement throughout the period 1985–2001, during which these poems were written. The comments of Natalie de Combray, Peter Fortunato, Kathleen Gemell, Mary Gilliland, Gail Holst-Warhaft, David McCann, Robert Morgan and Paul Muldoon were especially helpful, as were, since 1996, those of numerous members of the US1 Poets' Cooperative.

Versions of some of these poems have appeared in *Banyan, The Bookpress Quarterly, The Notre Dame Review, PN Review* and *US1 Worksheets.* An earlier draft of the collection was shortlisted for the Ernest Sandeen Award of the University of Notre Dame.

Contents

Sigodlin Poem   11

Time

Hadrian's Wall   15
Roskilde Fjord   17
Local Affairs   18
Stuttgart   24
Urban Renewal   25
Brigg   26
Musnikovo   34
The Dictator and the Dogs   36
InterCity   37
Selling the House   38

Place

The World's Oldest City   41
The Delegates Go to the Great Wall   43
Short Visits in Kyoto   47
Sravanabelagola   50
Eastern States
    Standard Time   52
    Hammond Hill   52
    Naif Painting   53
    Forebears   54
    Counting the Woodpile   55
Western States
    Mountain Time   56
    Death Valley   56
    Bah-vanda-sava-nu-kee   57
    Boiling River, Yellowstone Park   58
    Euphoric State, Berkeley, 1994   59

Entering the Cloud Layer

Forty-fifth Spring   63
Uncertainty Principle   65
Failure to Forget   67
Calling at the Wrong Address   69
Career   71
Irrational Fraction   73
Conference   74
Theory and Practice   75
The Garden Engineer   76
Four Flowers   78
'In this medieval house was born
    the modern novel . . .'   80
Welsh Interlude   82
Liszt at Midday, 1994   84
Musée Chagall   85
Deep Circulation   86
For Ilana, 1990   87
Entering the Cloud Layer   88

NOTES   91

Lighting the Steps

Sigodlin Poem

for Bob Morgan and my father

When I would cut the hedge in gaps
and lumps, and edge the lawn
or paint the narrow frame and window-ledge
unevenly, my father'd tell me
not to be cack-handed.

With that word at once an awkward hen
with small, bent hands would spring in view
and start to strut from side to side,
its twitching neck a frantic mimic
of what it was I couldn't rightly do.

And often now, when I have struggled
out of square with problems or with verse,
my father's voice comes back
in plain and ample confidence: 'No hurry.
And don't be so cack-handed.'

Time

Hadrian's Wall

A big wind shouts and smacks the trees
and thin clouds scoot for cover:
Northumbria blusters in and out,
rainsqualls stoop and shiver.

This weather bullies us for days,
twisting, interfering, snaps
and then withdraws. The ragged trees
and streams regain their shapes.

The Border lurches in a fitful light;
the Wall's squared stones define it still
though jumbled on the steeps of turf,
far from the world that fell.

Legions shod in silence crowd
the cropped grass of the barrack line;
their ghostly gear and weapons rattle
amid the month's dog-latin.

September frosts a stile, a web,
an auxiliary's moustache. From half
a mile the limestone gleams in focus,
and sun disturbs the mist like love.

Rare calm. Candescent day sweeps up
and clears the distances. Men mustering
dissolve to cloud and less, until
all that's left's a hawthorn, bracken,

path and shoulder up ahead:
a country's edge. Little strips
of meadow grace the fells, wall and hedge
make landscape's civitas. Levels under it

remain and form the same hill-sinew
that those new Romans, serving at
Empire's end, came all too well to know.
Their legions marched away and left

the land and people they had found,
subjects of boisterous wind and rain,
to make a living as they could
until another army came.

Roskilde Fjord

I

Given the skill
to burn and waste,
to bend and cut a perfect strake
and casually kill;

to stop their enemies
the longships' makers sank their craft
in the salt-fresh harbor mouth,
ribs raking the low tide.

II

Brought up from mud's preserve,
their peat-black hulls pronounce
an art and violence, alien commerce
we can only stop and wonder at.

Their captains also left us
place- and family-names;
a common hoard of speech
in by-road, field and fell.

Local Affairs

1 *Near Cambridge*

How she holds back, then floods and giddies us,
Dame Memory: her plump, patched hedges
rich in song, fen skies wide with the long
drone of insects and distant aircraft. Smoke
from garden fires sharpens, at a half-remove, the air.

This close and too-sweet island, whose halls
and chapels glow like honey in the failing light,
draws and hushes us. Behind cropped
and proper yews, we glimpse the hidden garden
entered once, if at all, and then as a child.

It seems close again. Even the tight, pale nettles,
clutched among hay stubble, catch at and repossess me.
Gestures first, then faces rise from the grass:
friends twenty years out of mind, their voices
England's own: light swelling from pent-up earth.

Quoin, buttress, mullion and corbel:
foursquare, the banks and colleges
stand on profits solid as themselves:
the scholarship of hops and wool.

Who occupies their rooms, if only for a while,
must shrive these masters' souls.
Their poor and peasantry had little part
in it: a lot not theirs to choose,

whose work doles out our privilege
and leisure yet. No theory sweetens
without it's well provided for
by merchandise, or government, or war.

The libraries and chapels rise
in delicate deliberation. Will such craft
and argument in fretted stone, redeem
each day's harsh work for it?

Rood screen, rose window, gilded tracery
came through the crash of battle; and stuff
of men's lives bought the masons' ale and bread,
who cut free these miracles of love.

East over Europe, over years, windows
glowed and dimmed and stayed unlit through war
and terror, and were made good after it.

This crippled street in Budapest, in Warsaw,
reveals a dozen periods, starting and ending
in the corners of each house. Every

square and alley recalls a hero – soldier,
poet, patriot – whose name has changed
as the demands of history change.

It's easy to wonder at régimes that in this way
demote or sanctify the past; too easy to forget
the history we choose defines us.

Retelling it we make our place:
a style reflexive as this courtyard's walls
turned in upon themselves, each course

incorporating what it has replaced.
Like cloudlight from gold leaf and fading saints,
the mind glides off such mass and fails to hold.

Most of what has fallen is rebuilt, becomes
an image of itself. What may seem square and neat –
the lives within too sheltered from the street –

are yet the substance of its every turn.
Those remembering may not all understand,
but who forgets has lost his place, his land.

IV *Theory*

Lifting from the last tower the light,
night explores the softly glowing town
and we turn from the window's blank,
from the real pitch and loss of grip –
gargoyles gaping, spires in the dark –
to what we can if only half begin
to solve: riddles and traditions of an art
so recently assumed; codes to be invented
or to break, a game of elegance and proof,
which keeps some distance off the void.

And while darkness slips out on the town
and westward across the island, and lights
flick and go out, doubt lifts and blows
among the papers, fear flickers in gaps
between houses, and we say, 'It is only the night,'
and think, if we question it at all, that
we are safe in our model of the world.
And the vision whispers and builds around us
softly, softly: a theory which so nearly fits
the facts, we shall soon have accounted for all.

v   *Study*

If I should stop to think about the pride
of knowledge and what ignorance is needed
to continue, will it be merely that, or go beyond?
Concern and care is not yet action.
Or if I knew, as much as one ever can,

that turmoil and compromise were a better part
than prudent argument, could I abandon it?
Theory and its practice are so sweet,
seeming all there is to stand on, at those times
when night hunts about the street.

The wind swings and claps about the street
with the racket of a loose steel sheet,
while shadows of late leavers from the bar
leap to the edge of the streetlamp's circle
and bound back quick at their walking feet.

(So it was the soul would reel out, in trance
or sleep, only to rein back lifelike
in the body's waking mass.) Feet scuff, rough
as cobbles, while the voices fade beyond sight
and hearing at the wall's grey limit.

Whether a country's or one man's memory;
our selves and their close histories entail us:
a present, pressing mass that lacks full sense,
but without which all's adrift and slides from focus:
shadows blustering on streetlit walls.

What profit if, at the desk, my world's neat portion
sharpens to a point? It is only the clear view
of omission. We should try instead to draw what lies
mostly behind the eyes. Outdoors, the dark
tightens and lightens and opens into day.

Stuttgart

'. . . die unheiligen jahren 1941 u. 1942 . . .'

A clutter of raucous sparrows
divides the pale wash of evening,
wheeling and diving as one to compose
anonymous black notes on the wire.
Closer, darkness presses the rose
and lilac's rain-heavy sprays
over the bench; their scents hold
the air still while the city roars

silently eastward, towards night. Single leaves
blur to a bush; the cultivated air lies down.
I salute the burgher and his civil dog
each evening as we meet. Beyond us, cobblestones
spiral out from the hilltop park, and lights prickle
the wooded hills gone grey, gone dark.

*   *   *

How far is this from the barrack block,
the waste of frost-pocked mud at the line's end?
In black and white, unlike our troubles now,
the screen shudders and sharpens to the clipped
diction of an old newsreel. The frame judders
over what there was: stick figures, shaved skulls,
and the city fathers: an impassive rank of broadcloth
brought to witness by the open pit.

The liberators collected the random living
and fired the huts, piled with their last freight,
leaving concrete, charred posts, towers, wire;
dust in the endless wind, floating like snow,
like blossom after rain, like hair, like ash,
like nothing left upon this earth.

Urban Renewal

The old streets have gone and the black town
centre's pointed, clean and priced beyond belief,
and the light without falls sweet on the green grain.

Summer breathes on the country. Tree crowns
unfold a cultivated picture of the place, where days
once lay down for years in the streets of a black town.

New plans overlie the locks and boarded station
but by the grey sheds the coal's grit leaves
still on my palm a few sharp, black grains.

Gardens among the docks and bricks cleaned of stains
have made *most desirable* these tall warehouse walls.
Even the street's names have changed in the new town.

Paint blisters on the last gate. Behind this one,
perhaps, stood a house, a room I called ours.
My fingers brush lightly the splintered grain,

and the street with its quite ordinary traffic returns
to eyes swimming against the sun, before which
old friends are gone from sight and the towns
turning to light fade with the golden grain.

Brigg

I

His mother's roses stood five and six feet tall
filling bed after weedless bed, with barely
a scape of moss or grass blade. In front
were silver birches – fifty, sixty feet – grown old:
with each big wind a branch or trunk came down.
Later, on the sawhorse in the spinney,
sawdust spurting from the crosscut's slot,
it was divided for the narrow fireplace.
The mossy, sodden wood dried slowly in the back bay
of the fuel shed, stacked on gritty cement, beside
coal, shouldered twice a year in hundredweights
by Barnes' men from his creaking lorry,
to make a shot-black cliff above the crouching child.

II

Small, mossy, twisted, old
apple and pear bore blemished fruits,
and most fell weeks early, softening
to sweetness in the orchard grass: bounty
for flies and wasps. From his dusty, pungent lair
under the redcurrant bush, fresh shoots and leaves
stitched out a particoloured sky. The afternoon
lay down about him; face pressed to earth,
he moved among an ants' and beetles' world.
Drought cracks springing between bare soil
invited a descent to Hades, where tall rocks
shivered and leaned towards the molten core
pictured in his Child's Encyclopædia.

III

Edith Holmes, née Lowson, was always propped
most properly among plumped pillows in
her dark, Victorian bed. We called each second
Sunday, after church. Pink and shrunk as her
crotcheted bed-jacket, she pressed my damp hand in
her knotted own. A fly batted behind drawn curtains
which swept the Turkey carpet. Her hair was carefully
    arranged
above the satin bows. Unseen for years, on a day of rare heat,
her garden throbbed outside. She asked me how was school.
The house was called *The Poplars*, although the trees
had long since gone, and I would take that long or longer
to see that this was the elegant Edwardian girl
by the door at West Farm, holding father's pony.

IV

At the town end of Bigby Street, his mother
and Mrs Foxton, shopping bags put down,
had set to talking. Their gossip curled
and bloomed into a world above his head,
each word familiar as her present hand
but the whole tale unguessable. 'Did you hear
who it was . . . What else *could* she have done . . . ?'
He circled, tugging and complaining, then let go
to stir a wad of leaves clogging the drain.
The noon train whistled through soft air; he felt
its wheels press down the crossing, underneath the voices.
Adult matters. Mrs F bent to chuckle at him. His mother
grasped his arm. Whose world could matter more?

V

The fireplace draws a child in winter
forgotten by parents, dozing in the warmth
long past bedtime. Lamps make foggy circles
out beyond the windows and drawn blinds.
But here soot-sparks wink moving kingdoms on
the firebrick back: castles, trains and waterfalls;
the child can bring them almost to the room,
closer than frost-beaded berries in the lane
through fields beyond the garden. Then coals subside,
stirring father and evening's end, transforming worlds.
The dining room and hall through which he has to go
are cold and dark. The heavy curtain jussles at the door
hinting of utterly other things without.

VI   *Second Form*

Headmistress' study held a dried elephant ear
in place of blackboard, propped upon an easel.
'Indian, not African.' She stood us by it to recite.
Its world of wrinkled valleys drove my answers out.
On the ground floor, behind the tallest door,
we memorised the carpet's muted edge.
Dawdling home, I came the long way by Pingley Farm,
ducking through tunnels leading to the front
near where uncle Arthur, riding dispatches from HQ,
was caught by a German patrol. Home at War's end,
he said he'd had to eat raw beets and monkey-meat
from the town zoo. His Great War became our First.
He winked. His false teeth grinned from ear to ear.

VII

The cows behind the house on Bigby Road
were hulks, moored or let to drift on mist
divided by a brook whose water carried
sluggish chalk-mud from the Wolds.
A half-sunk willow was a submarine
nosing into the cattle-wallow, green rods
gunning from its canted trunk. He was already
miles from home. From the conning tower
he marked an ash tree looming in the hedge
to starboard, calmly signalling *battle stations*,
then *full astern*. The diesels bubbled; salt water
thrashed and roiled abeam. Below his post
men sprinted down the echoing deck.

VIII

Marcus Thompson and our hero made stink bombs,
scouring Marcus' walled back garden for the right
ingredients: slug, worm segments, nuggets
of dog turd, a soft stew of wasps and flies
seethed in cider from the orchard trap. Behind a bed
of Marcus' mother's foxgloves, they assembled the device
in a cracked glass jar. Later they crept along
the backs of houses on St. Helen's Road to plant
and detonate it at Farrar's garage, moments before
he drove up, home from work. Another time
they seeped oil from a bent ten-gallon drum along
the playground slide. Marcus' father doubted
their story then as much as I wonder at it now.

IX

Chatty Binns was the town's simpleton –
'chatty,' from chat: a louse or nit –
a public charge, who'd beg all morning, then,
come midday, lounge outside the Angel Inn,
mouthing and gesturing in turn at the shoppers;
guzzling cold chips from yesterday's *Evening Star*.
He liked especially to ruffle the ready heads
of small boys as we straggled home from school;
his voice more violent but no stranger than
the shopman's or the banker's padded syllables.
I would cross to the North side of the market place
before it widened, to avoid the rank smell and all
his bellowed questions that had no earthly answers.

X

The Ancholme's new cut ran straight two mile
by the town's bottom edge, past Scawby Mill.
from point to soft mud point. On that stretch
fresh-painted yachts lay tight below the club.
He would explore the other, silted stream
past boats no longer needing mooring lines:
decks slanted, soft with moss, portholes open
to cabins of mute water. Where the river forked
and the island's ragged bushes round a shed
made no-man's-land, he'd crouch by the ribs
of a Humber Keel jutting from black mud, to plan
his sorties, Above his shoulder, miles of shining fields
and bolts of cloud unrolled and flapped against the sky.

XI *Near Sight*

I can't recall the age at which I realised
it wasn't usual to close one eye and lose everything
save the blurred edge of houses, friends, threats;
yet bring at once the beetle, cocked upon a leaf
five inches from my nose, to perfect focus.
I thought that anyone could, at will and in
this way, shut out the greater, swimming world.
Mine slipped in and out of focus at the garden's
ragged end, where pillows of half-clipped thorn
defended father's vegetables from Bowes' cows;
and the pungent smoke of a damped-down fire –
grass clippings, dead-headed roses, clots of weeds –
hung for days as I went out and straggled back.

XII *Boarders*

There was no privacy. Between class periods, boys
pushed and squabbled in packs: classmates, housemates,
intimate torturers. All night, a streetlamp glanced
through ranks of iron bed-frames, ghost-white
on whispered pacts and love affairs. Each morning
Matron snapped on the hanging bulb and twitched
the blankets from Sutton's bed, nearest the door.
We scuttled to the washroom's damp towels and drains.
The new-boy was cornered again behind the curtain.
Rain and mist had soaked the playing fields.
Searching for my name on lists, I prayed, with almost
as much fervor as the captains, for its absence.
Outside, perhaps, a kind of freedom could be had.

XIII

Released from school for an hour and
walking the city walls in slack, November light,
we saw four people burning a piano. An upright,
toppled on kindling. Old varnish flashed and boiled;
the strings went lax in thuds and curious shrieks.
A bottle made the rounds. We heard a fitful cheer.
We? I have a notion of companions, but can't imagine
who might have come on those long walks
escaping endless fellowship, or why this memory
should sieze me now at 3 am – four figures
in an afternoon beyond the moat – the music gone
that might have been performed, all traffic
momentarily still, on a wholly other continent.

XIV

They say one's childhood home – far fields
and nearer streets – are all (returning as
an adult) cramped and small. At first it seemed
just so; but now the smallest part has grown
to fill the flagstone terrace where the orchard
surely brushed against our windows once:
wet branches, leaves close-pressed as words.
It fades among fresh ranks of peonies and stocks.
Bowes' pasture's still beyond, though Bowes has gone.
His fields exhale thin scarves of mist; plashed hedges
pin them to the sodden ground. Faint cones of light
outline the roads that led away, and bring me back
to a small town I couldn't wait to leave.

XV

When May lies down among the too-lush leaves
maple, sumac, all having already swelled
to sweetness in early heat that drove out spring,
closing lines of sight and bringing
sharply to mind an older place
where overgrown and narrow lanes are pressed
between the quilted hedgerows, and shadows
populate a sky as changeable and muddled
as the past it shares . . . ; when May lies down
and sudden, foreign summer takes its part,
powdering the leaves with dust, I know that place,
being left to slip beyond the world's curve,
can never be one's own again, a home.

Musnikovo

1969

Three hours beyond Prizren I left
the border road, to find at evening an orchard:
dirt new-turned and soft under the buzzing leaves
and water threading to a stone basin.
It seemed a good place for the night.

And when the inevitable policeman arrived,
trying to move me on, this time it was
not for regulations' sake, but his concern
for *medved* – bears. He spoke excitedly, gesturing
toward the improbable, tree-crowded slope.

Had a bear *really* carried off a child? I was too tired
to believe in bears, and sensed he'd let me stay.
And yes, after we'd taken turns from a small flask,
he left, shrugging his shoulders, to walk
the chalk-dusted track to the village.

The children, who'd been hiding behind the wall
at our backs, then came out one by one, bringing
plums and blemished apples, and following much
whispering and noises off, gave me shyly a few
sweaty coins in a square of cloth 'to buy bread.'

They press around: Kosovars, Albanian and Serb;
hands rest a moment on my shoulder, their fingers
explore shirt and beard; the small, grave faces
push closer, eyes intent, almost to block the last light
from this page I cannot finish, nor put down.

1999

After the concert in Dubrovnik, and earlier, on
the bridge at Mostar, students spoke to me
of Njegos and his *Gorski Vijenac*: 'He is our Homer.'
Memories made powerful as rivers.
I had forgotten it, but wonder, now,

could these have been the same children,
grown into an age of change and visions,
who feasted here, each on his allotted portion?
Too early to come to this end, and to be sure
a frugal meal, but more than enough.

Under the sheltering trees and hedgerows
irregulars had gathered to reclaim their fields.
And on the voiceless, faceless fields, blackbirds
strutted, claws and beaks cocked on the leavings:
the clutter of shoes and plates and photographs,

the empty road, a tractor with tyres melted,
neighbours' hate sprayed on the stained cement
by steps leading to nothing, the view exact and clear
as the surviving frescoes at Pec: saints twisting
in torments behind the priests who could not

turn this aside: the haystacks burned or rotted,
hedges run riot with flowers, pruned trees loaded
with sweet, black plums; and just beyond the orchard wall,
a hundred meters square, perhaps a little less:
the field, the small fields of fresh-turned earth.

The Dictator and the Dogs

BUCHAREST, 1996

He dreamed a vast boulevard of heroes
fronted by flawless concrete, sweeping toward
The House of the People like a wave, the future

that will break over us all. And because they could,
his paragraphs leveled the untidy streets and houses:
nothing was left standing to chance.

His *Great People* would be rehoused
in rational blocks at the city's limits;
but no plan was made for the dogs.

Deprived of trees, cobbles, cracked seats, curbs
and fountains, the dogs were let go loose.
Not free. They would not leave their homes.

Ten years after, they still come each night
to steal back their city. From parks and dumps
and the palace garden, sectors now peopled

only in pictures, slipping grey but not as ghosts,
they come, canny as the new men. Singly or in packs,
living by snap and wit, they worry the past,

outlast revolution. Staying to be reckoned with,
glancing off our scent, they are becoming
our shadows in the flickering hour.

InterCity

The train investigates the backs of towns:
wagons, burning rubbish, dust
and lime. A factory someone owns
peels in the gritty waste.

The skies are blue as a giant's brush;
the day's unlooked for, indirect.
Square and scalloped gardens crouch
at their houses' backs.

Whitethorn, blackthorn, may and chalk,
a cutting swoops around us;
memory drops in place with a click
as if there were no loss,

Everything's recognisable here: nettles
crowding the canal's towpath,
wet clay printed by tractor tyres;
it comes back in a breath,

and scores of red 'phone-boxes
stacked sideways in a yard –
love or panic ghosted on their glass –
give up a rush of words

from a street corner in a black town
half a life and not ten miles away;
a voice tight with the unasked question,
the open line's hum in reply.

Selling the House

i.m. Robert Montague Holmes, 1903–1995

Rereading these letters, as if a first time,
beyond thirty years and all that's gone by: things
    we were leaning toward without knowing;
        how much can be recognised now?

Clearing the house now to be left a last time –
these eighteen years yours alone, never my home,
    but a place I could always come back
        towards – walls and roof contract and cool,

while the shortest day's sun slants low across
ditches and ice-skinned fields behind the fence.
    In front, trees that brought you the seasons
        give up their light and go out.

Night's thin comforter soon will fold over us,
in separate places, under the shifting clouds
    known only by an absence of stars.
        So winter calls everything down

and into itself, as you have drawn in your world.
Walks once shared become boundaries; the village,
    a narrowing garden, a single room. We are
        not far apart, yet you have turned

already towards the journey which will go
beyond the thread of letters, far out of reach
    and far beyond this: a small measure of thanks
        for my life and the half of yours you have shared.

Place

The World's Oldest City

Having a map which could at best
be called inadequate, his Turkish up to finding food,
Otel and Kamping, but not the (right) way,
he arrived, mid-morning, at a different Hüyük.

The goats and old men outside the teahouse
flurried to a new arrival, but no one knew
about 'old stones.' With several children,
gormless, witty, whooping ahead by turns,
and a student who had some French, he climbed
the Ak Dag to view the lake, dry soil, sparse groves
of birch and walnut, and over all of it transparant sky
propped on the village's patient, mud-brick back.
The wind from nowhere gathered its dusts
and galloped across the dun plain.

Afterwards, for hours in the café drinking tea,
he waited, watching the bus for Beysehir load animals
and people, wondering where was Çatal Hüyük:
the world's oldest city.
The student went to ask the teacher.

* * *

And now it is Kizan, that young schoolteacher,
exiled from Istanbul and Paris, eager to discuss
events outside, Vietnam, the revolutions of '68,
the Beatles – things as distant now for me
as she was from them then, having to veil herself
when she went out, whom I remember clearer
than those furrowed walls and pits and a little
coloured earth I came on two days after.

Kizan, and Ruhi and Ulvan who later
led me through the lush confusion
of village gardens, to poplars ranked
beneath a stony, pitted slope,
to a place where nothing old was left,
which was not Çatal Hüyük,
but where the wind muttered and glimmered
in evening's last swordburst of light.

The Delegates Go to the Great Wall

I

Manufactured in Japan, the minibus
is packed with us – distinguished visitors –
who set off, speaking of equations, spaces, spectra,
while villages bounce past in dust or tumble
up the chaotic, shaven hills, which suddenly
ten-roofed pagodas magical as fairy tales
punctuate with startling green tiles.

Bicycles and tottering, pedalled loads
of sand, cement, steel reinforcing-rods,
chickens, melons, TV-sets, caged crickets – pulled
and pushed by feet, hands, and the much-repaired
vehicles of those nations once most-favoured –
slow travel to a dusty crawl between
the perfect fields as small as living rooms,

which rooms here are smaller yet.
The hills are bulbous now and fields die out.
Few trees remain apart from those fresh-planted
in ordered rows against the stripping wind
that brings the Gobi's dust into Beijing and,
without those trees, would take its soil far East.
Look: up there now, the outcrops snap their teeth.

But no: it is the Wall! A dragon's backbone
zigzagged in calm sunlight on six thousand
li of hills: the edge of government and so
the very world. We are informed, with criticism
of the former ways but not without a certain pride,
that a mason's body, or a soldier's, or a peasant's
lies beneath each stone. And so we have arrived.

Minutes past the stalls of teeshirts, ivory, cloisonné
and Fujifilm, we are climbing, ladder-like, this Wall,
here populous with giggling families and soldiers
pictured, posed against the freshly-mortared blocks.
But just beyond the first watchtower's square,
slabs tilt into the earth between the unrestored
face walls, and crowds pass out of mind.

Only the wind, already in September cool,
perturbs a thousand miles of northern grass
bringing a murmur of the salt-pans and the desert.
Behind our backs the Middle Kingdom seethes
in plan and contradiction. Noon's coal dust settles
from a million cooking fires on the sultry courts
and gardens and the fantastic lions on the eaves.

II

Facing these northern hills that shade to blue,
it's easy to return a thousand years and be
a small official, a district magistrate once more
devoted to the law, sometime a dilettante
too fond of wine and art; perhaps a tax-collector,
part of the larger state: in any case, secure
within its boundaries that make of chaos, sense.

Or seem to. There is a process: axioms, evidence
assembled, proof and theorem follow. One must digest,
repeat the Classics, pass all exams, and (should the Heavens
will it) remain in favour, even prosper. Yet it is best
to stay some distance from the centre: powers sits
uneasily in the close air: a fit or freak of weather
can overthrow a generation's work and be one's end.

To the city-born this province is the end.
The Empire is the only order that I know.
The hills run off towards what has no name.
My opera is the wolf and crow. My former friends
address their rituals and policy a thousand miles away,
ignorant of the barbarians massing on the plain,
whose fires at night are many as the stars.

Exile and silence at this outpost on the Wall
have given need and means to think on what
has brought me here, what keeps this province
and its people scraping the wretched soil to yield
Lords and Emperor their share. Wall-soldiers
shiver in the autumn wind, but the ideals and all
the State's beliefs I have held close are colder still.

So let them go. But how then construe the world
and men without that one order? Better to keep it,
for 'the people are like children who must be so
corrected.' I can turn away or turn a closed eye
against 'unfortunate necessity,' who have helped
the Governor, my friend, sated after a fine meal,
judge a child who stole a cup of rice.

Loss and confusion tumble on the sudden wind,
rattling the cherry's leaves. A burst of rain darkens
the stones. If my page stay blank, or I should sit
too late, cold at the open window, it is to let
that chaos in which has no place as yet. Close
behind my back the rules unravel and a larger fate
takes shape to sweep us all towards the night.

Noon's heat resumes the air. Hermit, sage,
reformed Red Guard, peasant-capitalist and Commissar
prepare themselves for rest. In the Forbidden City,
in the Emperor's Hall of Time, exquisite instruments,
the regulators of affairs, his clocks, the gifts
of Kings and Tsars, stand stopped in dust,
the same that dries and cracks our lips today.

A chainsaw or a tractor irrupts and interrupts
this reverie and then the guides appear, gesticulating
to us to rejoin the group. Reconstructing, China makes
no room for solitaries, least of all among her visitors.
The bus and lunch and Thirteen Tombs will wait
no longer. Leaving the wind and empty hills behind,
we're taken on to see the crowded balance of our day.

Short Visits in Kyoto

Banker at Rokkaku Do

Briefcase set down, he
searches for coins and softly
tugs the bronze bell.

Heian Jingu Shrine

August's hot wind
disturbs the Gingko's shade
beyond paper walls.

Bamboo brushtrokes, pines
trained over two-foot mountains:
islands in the stream.

Gliding smears of ink,
the carp gulp together and
boil into our world

Nijo Castle

Each syllable creaks –
the chittering nightingale floor –
newcomer warning.

Parking

All night, vans and trucks
sit up and beg in front rooms
of wooden houses.

Appointment to Keep

Dumb, and blind to these
neon calligraphies, I
count streets carefully.

Narita Bus

A Gothick Kastle
as comic as we're foreign:
Tokyo Disneyland.

Business Lunch

Alley off a lane
off streets off Oike-dori:
a scrubbed oak door.

Behind the gate: tree
and cliff make ten perfect feet;
lunch open to view.

Noisily they eat
udon. No small talk. Without,
shoes and briefcase wait.

Sravanabelagola

We started barefoot, mixed among a snake
of murmurous pilgrims (shoes left for lost
at an over-eager sort of market-stall),
to straggle up the smooth, 300 meter rock:
grey pachyderm pushed up above the plain
and shouting, crowded, old, god-heavy land.

As we went up, concealing walls sloped out
to show the village tank; and dung and dust
and noise fell back, till one could pause and see
tin roofs winking up and down the street,
stagnant green canals, and fruit trees' straggled lines
smacked up against the palms and humps of hills.

Packed trains and buses lurch towards this omphalos;
psychedelic '60's trucks go wrong-way-wide
around blind curves, gears clashing, shouting
Ganeesha! – Horn OK! – Laxmi protect this one!
On every surface, wood and bulbous steel,
day-glo gods and mortals loll in paradise.

In the bazaar a tinsmith's soot-smeared boy
peers though torn curtains over racks of dippers,
milkcans large and small and tiffin boxes
crazy-piled above the sweeper's rancid slop.
His perfect teeth flash mockery and greeting,
redolent through two-stroke taxi haze.

And on the world's hill all the while the snake-coil
shuffles up: bent-headed, shrivelled, skipping in the sun.
Two memsahibs are trotted by in wicker chairs
borne up on knotted backs; their nervous laughter
ripples back and down across the undertow
of bare feet scuffing, slapping sun-warm stone.

On top, Gomateswara, naked and neatly coiffed
in studded whorls, swells through the open court
above coy cock and balls and down to toenails broad
as elephant-feet, all wreathed in scattered flowers,
bells and swells of muttered prayers, and Kodak
flashes through the holy smoke.

This is no peaceful place, you understand.
Laughing families picnic all around the court;
their shining teeth attack the simple food, although
devoutest ones among them wear gauze masks
so they should not ingest the smallest life.
Gomateswara stands impassively above, and smiles.

Coming down among new-swarming breezes,
pungent-sweet to counter thirst as scalped green coconuts,
we found our shoes perked up in proper ranks,
and once more shod, tugged back through the bazaar
and bobbing to the waiting bus, we heard taped voices
pronounce the thousand names of God, of gods, of god . . .

Eastern States

Standard Time

The room is whiter than the hour expects.
It was much too early to wake
when traffic stopped driving through sleep.

Tiptoeing on cold boards to the window, I see
disturbing silence rising through ice,
yards borderless, the street drawn in to a tree

suddenly strange, car-roofs soft and snow-rounded
as the slopes of a summer forty years gone,
when the sun shone, it seemed, always

and is still falling (no matter how harsh
and stone-cropped it was or has become)
on miles of bee-stitched, brilliant gorse.

Hammond Hill

Groping under racks and scarves of cloud,
the last light ruffles a fringe of trees,
silvering their cold, pale bark. A branch,
propped on another, goes off like a shot.

As night touches a face, a fringe of trees,
the whole wood leans in the windless air
propped on another, its branches become roots
spreading in the locked swell of soil.

The white wood strains in the windless air
as masts in a gale. Blue snowdrifts curl
eastward over the locked swell of soil
and cold retakes the pores of earth, of faces.

As masts stepping to a smart gale, the woods
hurtle, motionless, to darkness, last zero.
Cold resumes the earth's pores, and faces
huddle among scarves and coats and towns.

Naif Painting

The lake stretches and creaks under tattered snow,
its fabric made new for the season, drawn tight
this windless day as the same snappish air,
now silent, come summer, will tighten a sail.

Today the only presences gliding beyond the bridge
are skaters', and a dog surprised to a halt
on a snow-free patch. Behind their still shouts
a string of smoke uncoils and frays.

The random script that posed these figures
in arrested pirouettes – scarves extended
as the dog's tail – rolled out a flat of trees
against the startling, cloud-rinsed sky.

It stays us momentarily, who've lost
our footing in a fresh-glazed world.

Forebears

Nothing troubles a ghost town
whose silvered houses crouch against the wind.
Leaves twist across the gritty ends of snow
smudging a roadside leading somewhere else.

The families whose these houses were,
are insubstantial now as air. Walking
under their trees and gable ends,
they knew the fields and saw them taken.

Without these people and their chosen words,
'what' would swallow stone and board;
trees without names would hide the road,
dirt stop wells and cellar doors,

rain take table, lintel, roof.
Their speech is all we have, or most of it;
voices lending corners to the square,
picking their stories out of absent air.

Counting the Woodpile

When winter cracks like a gun
in the bleached woods
and garden and stream are stone,
we'll begin to burn

the fifty summers cut and split
and stacked last fall. It'll take
all that to keep the old man out
until the next.

When the wind kicks at the door
and the window's thick with ice
inside, we'll wonder how much more
can hold through March.

The years of sun and growth
leave threads only of ash and smoke:
a play of light and warmth.
Enough. Almost enough.

Western States

Mountain Time

In Oak Creek Canyon, Arizona, minutes
from the highway, ethnic restaurants and galleries
of *Original Western Art*, seven whole ages
reach and stand apart. Not ours; a thousand feet
of time set out in sand, in lime. Sweet
pine and Gambel's oak, moss overlays
old ripples and the long laying down of seas,
the quicker prints of rain and mist.

Here and all across the West, sandstone,
pumice – shattered blinks and twitches
of an order shifting under – bare their bones.
Three hundred or ten thousand years of signatures
make little difference. Who would shout and fight
and build a silly breath, a whisper, shadow on the grass?

Death Valley

Will it be hot or cold or simply like
this endless flootlit distance where eyes
skip and swerve to the least detail –

    mica, orestone, twisted bolts and plate,
    bone-white beams that make
    this wilderness emptier far than if
    the miners never had been here –

or will death be, as the lives that led to it,
provisional as ourselves, their silly bearers:
a mirage of drive-in banks and grocery marts?

Here is a kind of end – shimmering rockface,
boulders, trees one can't resolve, wavering
in a grace of heat and dust – devils blowing
and tumbling at the edge of sight.

Bah-vanda-sava-nu-kee

or, INDIAN GEORGE WATCHES THE EMIGRANTS

Boy-who-runs-away had seen them start
and struggle up the dry stream bed,
leaving the last green flash of cottonwoods:

a distant, ragged, dogged people: blue and grey,
rocking their parched wagons over the sand ledges
toward the impassible cliffs they could not see.

(He stayed in hiding, prudently. Young men, returning
to his village, said the yellow-heads had sticks
could split the air, throwing death a distance.)

He watched and watched them out of sight, who might
have led them out. Did then the empty vista –
magenta cliffs, shimmering cinder cones,

slopes in strict repose: all that present landscape
furrowed by the element they would die for want of –
wheel across his flat, brown eyes?

Boiling River, Yellowstone Park

for Marcy Barge and Russ Walker, December 1987

By vague ranges shouldering the clouds,
through Paradise under a meagre scrim of snow,
we drove to where the Gardiner River licked its rocks
and bitter grass and every branch was bleached.

Outside the car, the air snapped and cut at us
and at a quarter mile the hot spring's steam
peeled off and flattened over the bank's
carved edge to tear and vanish, icing the last leaves.

'Undressing's much the worst,' you said. I doubted it,
but, once among the roil of eddies, cold and hot
by turns, and under the low cave, sweet

in mineral summer, strange was real.
Snow-parched sage and mountain blurred to steam.
The old year died as zero crystallized our hair.

Euphoric State, Berkeley, 1994
with apologies to David Lodge

Jays argue raucously and swoop among
the eucalyptus castles of the trees,
and bushes scramble where the grass has gone
up hillsides tilted through absurd degrees.

The campus shimmers in a sprightly air:
it is all *things*: stone benches, walks and posts.
Ideas seem shyer than a snowflake here.
The buildings are too square and grand for us:

all frightful towers, windows tall for giants
leaning toward the city on their sills;
huge bay picked out with boats and islands;
inhuman swath of golden light and steel:

the bridge connecting mist to land
that at this distance seems to carry nothing
on its always-being-painted orange span,
beyond which greater mists have shelved the sun.

Fog permeates the mind and morning air,
makes quite impossible the task at hand:
to think here and to write with proper care
will be as difficult as life elsewhere.

Entering the Cloud Layer

Forty-fifth Spring

Dawn's kerosene pooled on the runway.

Sleepless after a night's travel,
I nod in the train's sluggish heat.

As it leaves the city, spinneys and windbreaks
lean into light. The line shrugs and straightens
towards the Pennines. I come back always to this.

Older and calmer perhaps, eyes closing
more readily — but how much has changed?
Beyond routine, truth is shy as ever; is chiefly
learning how little one knows.

The hedgerow's a world's edge;
no: a world itself, opening to the damp air,
a trouble of green sprinkling the copse,
ploughed fields rich and ruffled as silk
wrapped foursquare about farms.

From the train's streaked window,
the scrubbed stone of Victorian stations.
cast iron sparkling on gutters, bossed railings,
names fresh-planted in flowers: mill towns clean
as the passing whistle. Watch how, beyond the last
house in the upended street, the whole sky opens.

*   *   *

Clean because idle, millwrights long gone;
still pinned in valleys by smokeless chimneys,
the towns show faces like a family in the front parlour,
scrubbed for the holiday visits, children fidgeting
on newly-waxed furniture, beneath the inlaid daggers
our Dad brought back from the war.

Millstone gives over to limestone, the outcrops
whiten eastward as the valley opens
to rough pastures where faded and fresh
graffiti – KOP RULES, *Faggot*, MANchester,
LEEDS FC – bully the drifting sheep.

A raw wind sweeps old papers and leaves
against hedges, banks and culverts, as if
to tidy up the spate of words with which I can't say
where we're going, or how fast, or far.

Clouds scurry across midmorning's sky
as the track unrolls from the hills.
A glasshouse winks two fields beyond the road.

The picture's perfect and it makes
no earthly common sense.

Day's light pours over everything.

Uncertainty Principle

for David McCann

Stepping late from the dark sedan, leaving behind
sleepers stirring at open windows, she crosses
to the far side and follows four streets
to where the last ends in a half-lit wall.

Here are the two steps down to a low door
which opens as she knew it must. Inside,
across a garden where lilies gleam and murmur
in the light current, she will see others coming,

crossing the bridge and drenched lawns,
the hems of their dresses dark with dew.
Starlight glisters from glass and scattered plate.
The summerhouse tinkles with wit.

Voices acclaim a new arrival, lanterns
nodding from branches far over the water
where boats carelessly verge towards
what kind of midnight, of crowds?

They are as bright and many as the stars:
quick movements in the corner of an eye
ceasing the instant her head turns.
A spoon winks and is lost in the grass.

What does she taste, later, standing rumpled
and dusty outside the closed door? An echo
troubles the air. As first light shifts and breaks,
the long car noses down the street, and,

another door clicked shut, moves off past empty lots,
charred shells of buildings, waste lumber, trash,
excrement, and through it, pale trees rooting
and sunflowers tugging at the stale breeze.

Failure to Forget

after A.R. Luria: The Mind of a Mnemonist

S's mind flocked with images: each word
called up a vivid history. For instance,
heat was the heavy summer of '13, wind
limping at the swollen curtain by his bed,
a German doctor who coughed discreetly,
pronouncing the illness 'minor . . . in his head.'

Curtains with a tasseled border brushed his head,
Flocked wallpaper folded forever on the word
as he began to embroider that sharp instance:
fever at once made tangible by the wind
which barely ruffles the flowers in their beds
beneath his window where they nod discreetly.

The rest of the sentence plucks discreetly
at his sleeve. The doctor's cuffs move overhead,
splashing the dusk to emphasise a word.
He will not wonder yet at this small instance
of how things twist among themselves and wind
around his mind. He fidgets in the straightened bed.

Mid-sentence, years later, heat returns him to that bed
as the summer's shouting flowers indiscreetly
clamour on curtain and wallpaper, obscuring the heads
before him and even his friend's, whose word
conjured this memory and claimed the instant.
Minutes lag, barely lightened by the wind.

If only, he wonders, when again he can, the wind
would cuff it all to shreds, like steam; but the narrow bed
is always waiting for him, curtained discreetly

and made up in the corner of each day. Although no head
save his turns at the soft implosion of the word,
all the world he has, flows from that instant.

And is it ever in perspective? An instant
of confusion rattles the window, colours wind
up and the glass parts, like a river over its bed.
His reflections shiver and join indiscreetly
to make up an unruly scene somewhere ahead.
With a last effort, he pronounces the word

heat, trying for the word only, with no instance
of the wind's force. Without success. The child's bed
and all it led to stands discrete and present in his head.

Calling at the Wrong Address

Walking past the hundredth high oak door,
under its monogram illegible today at noon,
one might step aside with half a thought and enter
a cobbled court that seems familiar . . .

*   *   *

But something tugs at us and comes between
to overlay the present, softer scene;
each day being a mind's eye swimming
with houses built on houses like the clouds
that tower and purple into storm
under some quite distant, crackling sky.

A place that still surprises us –
although it's fast becoming home,
and where, it's said, the central fact is space –
might seem a most appealing prospect,
but is, alas, part-true, if even that.
Nothing *is* unless it's lodged in time.
Time makes space for us, then takes it back.

*   *   *

The lower lead-roofed buildings drip
on plants set out beneath the concierge's window;
her face swims up behind lace curtains,
hostile, but too curious to stop me yet.

Above it: balconies, tall windows shortening
floor by floor, slate gables, chimneys,
boat-shaped roofs that float and fade
in bags of wrinkled cloud.

*   *   *

Go on and through, then hesitate beyond
the second stairway . . . should it be the third?
Wide, shallow steps, waxed oak
and threadbare carpets point toward
what might have been remembered, given time:
uneven plaster in the niche, where damp
has worked a half-forgotten map.
All as comforting to someone's eyes
as slippers or a chair, but utterly
and still minutely strange to one
who wonders, halted on the stair,
what other futures might be playing now,
and sees the border where the carpet ends
is ridged with years of paint,
and steps are narrower from here.

*   *   *

Reaching the landing with its empty vase
and rain-streaked window, the door
is standing open, as it would have been,
to let pass gusts of muffled conversation,
music, laughter like a laden tray
carried warm from kitchen out to guests:
snatches of a life unwoven, to be made up fresh.

The voices swell and sweep and fade
as radio waves that ghost at evening
suddenly halt and start,
lighting the few short steps
dividing day from night,
what happened from
what might have been.

Career

He always thought the word 'career'
meant headlong downhill progress, half
out-of-control, so that one barely made it
around the corner by the hardware shop
and over the narrow bridge, pavements
slicker than a frozen dewpond, runners
squealing against the chipped kerb.

One's principles have little to do with it.
Others might have chosen theirs, but his
career came over him like a kind of weather
which the merest breath could have changed
entirely, though now it seems impossible
it could have been otherwise, so quickly
we forget what might have been:

doors unopened, fields left far behind,
a prospect fading half way over into mist
and rain. Yet he is, he's eager to insist, lucky
to have been dropped and now be so absorbed
in this strange calm and trouble, with all its care
for detail and bizarre side-issues. He's enthralled
to try the puzzles fate assigns each week,

although he cannot tell if they are set
by the Gods of order who already know the score
and sit, grumbling and exchanging bets on who
might give the least annoying answer; or are
his own devices, dreams; or if they grow among
that common ground which all those earlier visitors
have beaten and defined: his discipline.

The road unravels and he gathers speed again,
leaving the little clamour and the lights behind,
now pitching between close walls of rock.
The whole air's warming up. Piñon pines
and mesas loom under a shaken bag of stars.
Between avoiding outcrops and the edge, I wonder
that he should, so far, have fallen mostly on his feet.

Irrational Fraction

When it seems that part of my life
    must have belonged to another, someone
        more suitable, deserving what notice

has fallen my way and knowing precisely what to do
    next; it's as if I woke half way here, to days
        couched in these alien symbols

with which I might pretend a certain facility,
    adept at seeming to manage them,
        but not (it now becomes clear) well;

for I find myself walking on stage to applause
    from the darkened hall, bowing, and about to sit
        at the open instrument, innocent of every note.

Conference

In the Douanier's carnival night
the trees are perfect, spare and bright
and leafless as our winter speech.

Two figures stand in foreground,
their silks are thin against the air;
a moment more and they have gone.

December's heatless sun
faces frost on lawn and wood,
while in the lecture hall we coax

a minute world of care and proof
directed on quite other fields,
bearing neither bud nor leaf.

And yet a stir runs in the room,
for something has been done
perhaps as startling as breath;

at such a moment everything
is suddenly charged and very clear:
there is no other path to take.

But all the ordinary days,
uncovering only what's allowed,
one may still regret the loss

when broad day shimmers and there are
no figures dressed for carnival or not
on heartless lawns that brim with light.

Theory and Practice

Leonardo's fabulous machines
in metalpoint and pen and softly washed
flex and flap their varnished wings.

Suspended under or within them, knuckelled,
near-bewitched, thought-pilots pedal the mind's air;
their small, bound figures furiously churn or row

with forces greater than his theories would allow,
but every struggle's fitted neatly to the page
among capstans, angels, levers, blocks and flowers.

'I can master water or the whirlwind's rage,
fix likenesses in bronze, on walls, in wood;
I have built winches, cranes and cannonades

to satisfy a Prince's every wish. I can
interrogate the least element of nature's art,
and plot the vortices of river, age or heart.'

The contract gained, decked with honours due,
he will retire to a crabbed solitude
and cultivation of those arts which quite belie
these grand and foolish claims.

The Garden Engineer

Water will be your greatest challenge:
an intractible medium to be coaxed
sometimes miles and given the precise head
to overcome running losses and at the end
raise a perfect fan over Neptune's car.

You must make pools to hold Narcissus' face
long after he goes; mirrors changeable as the sky,
cascades which slip like silk across their lips,
and others: a broken-backed sliver of light
deep under leaves in Diana's grove.

You will need valves and sluices to drain it
for those Northern winters, when the valley's edge
swoops to the bare quincunx, and frost uncolours
the lawns and raked alleys. How different from
our comfortable mists, where moss pads out the year!

You must learn to level this and raise that
with a hundred cartloads of boulders and earth
as He dictates, to hide or reveal a distant tower,
make way for a maze and summer houses
where favourites can be met unobserved.

You will imagine tall trees catching a wind that stills
among their million leaves, leaving shade
penned under them in pools where He might weigh
the little countries and the great, and so determine
matters of state among your tended beds.

Thus, my young friend, cultivate most carefully
technique and beauty, detail and the grand design;
quicken your skills by all means to match His
passing pleasures, but look beyond a King's whim.
It may last half a lifetime; your garden: centuries.

Four Flowers

Toadshade

Named not for its broad triplets
of fleshy leaves and short, erect bud
unfolding to a ragged star on the wood's floor;
but rather for its propensity
for moist and shady places
where small acts of violence
may be safely hidden.

Its polite name is trillium.

Viper's Bugloss

Alien. A bristly plant
with short, claw-like stems,
each bearing a single bloom.
Colonises roadsides and waste places.
Of the family: *Forget-me-not.*

Sky Lupine

Favours weak and stony upland soils.
A widespread root system generally
keeps this roadside escape secure against
rising into the egg-thin, blue horizon.

Erythonium Americanum

Pale leaves brown-birthmarked,
shielded yellow petals freckle,
nodding in the half-shade.

Trout-lily turns to adder's tongue.
What beads of dew or poison
a simple name puts on.

'In this medieval house was born the modern novel . . .'

In course of building work in London, 1969,
workers found five skeletons, one of whose skulls
had been trepanned. Being also *uncommon small*,
it was thought likely this was Lawrence Sterne's.

(For after death in lodgings in New Bond Street,
his body was reported snatched by resurrection men
and sold to the anatomists at Cambridge, where,
upon public dissection, the face was recognised too late.)

But whether his or not, and incomplete, the bones
were taken north to be reburied in Coxwold Parish
where they now lie two yards outside the church door
under a cracked and partly faceless stone.

Inside the church – too elegant it seems for this
small village – are oak box-pews, foursquare,
whose doors secure with neat brass latches:
one cannot slip in or quietly out of here.

A leaflet written by the present vicar
informs us that, during his incumbency in seventeen-
sixty-two or three, Parson Sterne had these pews made,
and further, that their height was, earlier

this present century, *reduced* by cutting
several inches from their lower halves. For many
of his congregation, weekly sermons were their sole
diversion. What walls he made to keep them still!

Did he harangue them, Sunday captives, with his
peculiar wit? And afterwards, would he retire home
to take up argument behind squat chimney-breasts,
return to chapters upon sleep, or button holes,

the paths of musket balls, a promontory of noses –
his burgeoning book, opinions hodge-podged,
various and colourful as his liberal meals?
Mossy walls wrap tight about his apple trees

which today must be imagined, for walls are high
and house and grounds are closed, under a wind-scarred sky.
And look: his congregations are dispersed,
the windows dark and cold. The end is here.

Welsh Interlude

for Bill and Dilys McCann

Abertafol

Between the mottled ebb and landward ridge –
slate banked and crumbled over cottage row –
this tannery turned to tearoom's now
your home, its garden tilted side over edge
over end: an eaves-high, roof-high wedge
of holly, laurel and rose. Terraces
overflow with flowers, pools and arbours press
the gable ends; from there, and window ledges,
martins barely leave off bombing your doorstep
to launch their sorties over Tafol and Dyfi
and slow-turning, sand-bearing sea.
As day draws in, the light slides north and west,
far from some of the swarming voices, here,
to bring your world to temporary rest.

Llyn Barfog

Futures unexpected as this sky
sweep open over valley, house and bridge.
Heat streams up on the climb to the hidden lake,
today unbearded, stitched with dragonflies
and lily-blue: such untroubled greys,
expansive, quiet green. Bracken fronds
are laced around the panel's *art nouveau*
and nettle stalks are clustered by the fence.
The breath's invisible on Cader Idris
and evil stones lie silent in the sun.
Words are growing at the pace of moss;
their meanings still may open if we wait.
For days the kobold's knocking can't be heard,
and nothing's caught between the wires but wind.

Liszt at Midday, 1994

for Adam Fellegi, Zichy Jenó 41, Budapest

Darkness and loss
he brings us   time in his hands
while midnight chords swoop
to the high windows

Hands that precisely let fall
flickers of stormlight in balance
then harsh shouts once more
Satan thumping the table

The reply comes   pale as leaves
stripped against a bruised sky
fifty years swept into the air
in gusts of sudden light

Musée Chagall

Separating earth and heaven, this green
bubble of sustaining, skin-deep air
is all we know. Inhale and hold a breath.
Chasms gulp and stretch on either hand.

Histories that might have held us still
are at the end substantial as his clouds'
bunched air, which hides and colours and reveals
our dreams: ladders, music, swaying crowds;

the bride who gathered the folds of her dress
and floated above the bumbling village
as rosy heat settled on the place,
setting the heart's hidden ones on edge.

Palaces and kingdoms shimmer, attaining less
structure than clouds themselves, dreams or houses
seen once, to be recalled imperfectly and fade,
leaving just enough to taunt us with their loss.

Or, should they return, it's as a rainbow's sweep
bending sky to earth, which quickly softens
and is gone. In the east the night sky plumps
and purples like a bruise. Stormlight gains.

Doves and roses wait, the steep-terraced olives;
bushes wait to burn, rocks to be cleft: all expect
the magical to happen. A small wind freshens
the patient fruit, the path that leads us out.

Deep Circulation

What has been done cannot be taken back.
The water sinks and vanishes from sight
bearing traces of the things we did not lack.

Salt tilts the parcels that dissolve and pack
half lives of strontium dust, intangible as light,
as what's gone down and can't be taken back.

Ice-blue as cobalt, laced molecules in dark
cold cells turn over to the pitch of night
their balances of what we did not lack.

Five hundred years ahead those elements will break
a different ocean's surface, holding tight
their histories that no one can take back.

Part-spent lives will gather in the slack
between tides, at their appointed site,
immaculate as all we did not lack.

The simple water plays against the dock,
preserving every theft and careless gift:
what we have done cannot be taken back,
nor any comfort that we would not lack.

For Ilana, 1990

Our smallest daughter said
that all night dreaming filled her head,
keeping her warmer than the covers
bunched about her bed.

Why not? When she's awake,
from rooms apart we hear her busy voice
building another family with all its troubled love
and complicated noise.

Entering the Cloud Layer

As flaps go down and the engines throttle back,
    tilting into the cloud tops,
        I know the exact moment when,

breaking the double window-glass, I could
    burst out and jump that forty feet
        to land half-stunned on vaporous cliffs,

their turf as springy as a California lawn.
    Brash song excites the hedges in that street
        where shadow columns tilt across a wall

from grounds of a house set back too far
    among white leaves substantial in the air:
        a world in negative, steaming before the rain.

It's as if a future held in trust and closed
    were suddenly divided to allow one past,
        and entering, I'd straighten to look up

from that other place, past shifting coasts and bays,
    into the wholly-polished, clear absence
        we're still descending through.

Notes

11 *Sigodlin Poem*: 'sigodlin' means out-of-square or crooked, as in poor carpentry. I learned the word from Robert Morgan's poem of the same name. As a child, it never occurred to me that 'cackhanded' was probably derived from 'caca.'

17 *Roskilde Fjord*: five Viking ships were raised from the mud of Roskilde Fjord in Eastern Zealand, Denmark, during the 1960's.

24 *Stuttgart*: the epigraph is taken from the text on a memorial to the Jews of Stuttgart.

26 *Brigg*: a small market town in North Lincolnshire (now called South Humberside), England. In part I, a spinney is a small planting of trees; in VI, 'second form' (UK) = 'second grade' (US); in VII, the Wolds are a low range of hills.

34 *Musnikovo*: a village, some distance south of Prizren, in Kosovo, which I cannot locate on my maps. Petar II Petrovic Njegos (1813–51) was a Montenegrin *vladika* or prince-bishop and the author of *Gorski vijenac* (The Mountain Garland, 1847). He was regarded as an enlightened ruler and admired as a poet.

41 *The World's Oldest City*: Çatal Hüyük, or Çatalhüyük, near Çumra in Konya Province, Turkey, is the site of a neolithic settlement that flourished 5,000–6,000 years ago. For a time it was the oldest known city settlement.

47 *Short Visits in Kyoto*: *udon* (Japanese) is a kind of noodle.

50 *Sravanabelagola* is the site of a Jain temple in Karnataka State, South India. Gomateswara is a Jain 'saint.'

57 *Bah-vanda-sava-nu-kee* ('boy-who-runs-away'): the name of a Shoshone, also known as Indian George, who, in 1849, watched settlers and gold-seekers struggling to find a way out of Death Valley. His photograph, taken in the 1930s, appears in *Twilight of the Jackass Prospectors* by Robert Ansel Cartter and George R. Cartter, Sagebrush Press, Morongo Valley, CA 92256.

80 *'In this medieval house was born . . .'*: Lawrence Sterne (1713–1768) took holy orders and was vicar of Sutton-on-the-Forest, near York, for twenty years. In 1759, after publication of the first two volumes of *Tristram Shandy*, he became famous and, being presented with the parish of Coxwold, near Helmsley in North Yorkshire, he retired there to live in Shandy Hall. The title is taken from a plaque at that house, but is not strictly accurate, for the book was conceived and begun some time before his move there.

New and Recent Poetry from Anvil

Gavin Bantock
Just Think of It

Oliver Bernard
Verse &c.

Nina Bogin
The Winter Orchards

Dick Davis
Belonging

Harry Guest
A Puzzling Harvest
COLLECTED POEMS 1955–2000

Michael Hamburger
From a Diary of Non-Events

James Harpur
Oracle Bones

Anthony Howell
Selected Poems

Peter Levi
Viriditas

Gabriel Levin
Ostraca

E A Markham
A Rough Climate

Dennis O'Driscoll
Exemplary Damages

Sally Purcell
Collected Poems

Daniel Weissbort
Letters to Ted

Some Poetry in translation from Anvil

Josep Carner: *Nabí*
Translated by J L Gili

Nikos Gatsos: *Amorgos*
Translated by Sally Purcell

Goethe: *Roman Elegies* and other poems
Translated by Michael Hamburger

Nikolay Gumilyov: *The Pillar of Fire*
Translated by Richard McKane

Yehuda Halevi: *Poems from the Diwan*
Translated by Gabriel Levin

Nâzım Hikmet: *Beyond the Walls*
Translated by Ruth Christie and Richard McKane

Poems of Jules Laforgue
Translated by Peter Dale

Ivan V. Lalić: *Fading Contact*
Translated by Francis R Jones

Federico García Lorca: *A Season in Granada*
Edited and translated by Christopher Maurer

Vasko Popa: *Collected Poems*
Translated by Anne Pennington and Francis R Jones

Rainer Maria Rilke: *Turning-Point*
Translated by Michael Hamburger

Poems of François Villon
Translated by Peter Dale

Rabindranath Tagore
Song Offerings
(Gitanjali)
Translated by Joe Winter